Bubbly

# Bubbly

Jonathan Ray

RYLAND
PETERS
& SMALL
London  New York

DESIGNER **Sailesh Patel**
EDITORIAL ASSISTANT **Miriam Hyslop**
LOCATION RESEARCH MANAGER **Kate Brunt**
PRODUCTION **Gavin Bradshaw**
ART DIRECTOR **Gabriella Le Grazie**
PUBLISHING DIRECTOR **Alison Starling**

First published in the United Kingdom in 2001
by Ryland Peters & Small
Kirkman House, 12–14 Whitfield Street,
London W1T 2RP
www.rylandpeters.com

10 9 8 7 6 5 4 3 2 1

Text © Jonathan Ray 2001
Design and photographs
© Ryland Peters & Small 2001

ISBN 1 84172 185 9

Printed
and bound
in China.

A CIP record for this
book is available from
the British Library.

# contents

CHAMPAGNE
BRUT

*Cuvée*

*Joséphine*

*Joseph Perrier fils & Cie*

what's all the fuss about fizz?

It may only be a glass of fermented grape juice with a few bubbles in it, but imagine how flat a celebration would be without fizz, poo, pop, champers or bubbly…

The term 'sparkling wine' refers to any wine which contains bubbles of carbon dioxide, the most revered example of which is called champagne. Although in truth it is no more than this, bubbly is special: poems have

# CELEBRATION!

been written about it, songs sung about it, and it is synonymous with celebrations and gaiety. It is inconceivable to think of acclaiming a new-born, commemorating a victory or saluting the New Year without a bottle of bubbly. And what on earth would playboys sup from starlets' slippers other than frothsome fizz?

There is never a wrong time for a glass of bubbly: simply uncork a bottle and you immediately elevate a gathering into a party. Asked on what occasions she would take champagne, the late Madame Bollinger famously replied: 'I drink it when I'm happy and when I'm sad. Sometimes I drink it when I'm alone. When I have company I consider it obligatory. I trifle with it if I'm not hungry and drink it when I am. Otherwise I never touch it – unless I'm thirsty.'

just a little
bit of history

It doesn't do to make a big thing about it when in a room with French people, but there is some evidence to suggest that it was the British who invented champagne.

Up until the late 1600s wine made in Champagne was still, French glass being too weak to make bottles strong enough to contain sparkling wine, and cork stoppers being a thing of the future. The English on the other hand, were already using cork bungs in their bottles as well as having perfected making glass strong enough to confine fizzy wine. There is also evidence that the English were in the habit of adding sugar to imported wines - notably those from Champagne - to make them sparkle, some twenty years or so before the Champenois had worked out how to make their wine fizzy. On the other hand, there are those who claim that Blanquette de Limoux, a fine sparkler made in the south of France, pre-dates sparkling champagne production by some 150 years. Wherever or however it was invented, it soon became apparent that the soil, climate and choice of grapes in Champagne were ideal for the production of bubbly. Even though it is now made all over the world, from Argentina to England, from India to New Zealand, the only sparkling wine entitled to call itself champagne is that which is made in the region of

that name, using
no grapes other
than Chardonnay,
Pinot Meunier and
Pinot Noir by the
reputable Méthode
Champenoise.

The vineyards of the Champagne region are the most northerly in France and the grapes have difficulty ripening fully, leaving them high in acidity and low in

# SO GLAMOROUS!

flavour – ideal for winemakers seeking to achieve the austere, elegant style characteristic of the best champagnes. Unlike in the New World, biting frosts and hail storms can affect the quality of each year's harvest dramatically, and as a result 80% of production is devoted to non-vintage champagne.

Champagne comprises only a fraction of the total production of sparkling wine, but our fondness for it is clear, given that 320 million bottles are consumed around the world every year.

Although other sparkling wines might be made from such varieties as Chenin Blanc, Muscat, Müller-Thurgau, Aligoté, Clairette, Riesling, and Pinot Blanc, champagne may only be made from Chardonnay (sometimes used on its  own to make **blanc de blancs**) – and two red grapes, Pinot Noir (best-known for making red burgundy) and its close relative, Pinot Meunier, a grape little seen elsewhere, but highly prized here for adding fruit and acidity to the champagne blend. Despite being red grapes, these last two varieties are sometimes used without Chardonnay to make a white champagne (**blanc de noirs**).

# why bubbly
# is bubbly

Méthode Champenoise is the most successful process used to make wine fizzy. Most top-quality sparkling wines and all champagnes are produced this way.

Grapes are picked and pressed and the resulting juice undergoes an initial fermentation - usually in stainless steel tanks - although some producers prefer to use oak barrels. Once fermented, the wines (which may be from different vintages, vineyards and grapes) are blended together. Before bottling, an additional solution of yeast, sugar and wine (**liqueur de tirage**) is added, causing a second fermentation in the bottle which produces the bubbles.

Sealed with crown caps, the bottles mature on their sides for up to three years, after which they are regularly turned and gradually tilted - or 'riddled' (**remuage**) - until vertical, causing the sediment created during the second fermentation to fall into the neck of the bottle. The necks are frozen and the icy pellet of sediment is expelled by removing the cap - the pressure of the fizzy wine forcing the icy plug out (**dégorgement**). Prior to corking and labelling, a mixture of wine and sugar (**liqueur d'expédition**)

is introduced to the bottle (**dosage**). An alternative system which is often used to produce sparkling wines is known as the **Transfer Method**. Wines that have undergone their second fermentation in the bottle are disgorged under pressure into tanks – the whole contents, not just a frozen plug – prior to filtering and rebottling. This method is widely used in the New World, and it produces very decent wines, albeit without the finesse and elegance of those made by the **Méthode Champenoise**. This is a much less expensive process as it removes the time-consuming 'riddling' and the costly freezing, disgorging and topping up of each bottle individually.

The **Tank Method**, also known as the **Cuve Close** or the **Charmat Process** involves a second fermentation in a sealed tank rather than in a bottle. Most German Sekt is made this way which, whilst good, doesn't have such

# MAKING THE BUBBLES

fine or long-lasting bubbles as wines that are made by the previous methods. **Carbonation** is the cheapest and least effective method of injecting bubbles into wine via what the French jokingly refer to as a **pompe bicyclette**.

something
for everyone

Champagne commands a premium, sometimes unfairly. Without doubt a well-made sparkling wine from anywhere else is preferable to a poorly-made champagne.

Champagne is generally marketed under brand names, amongst the best-known of which are Bollinger, Gosset, Jacquesson, Krug, Moët & Chandon, Mumm, Pol Roger, Louis Roederer, Ruinart, Salon, Taittinger and Veuve Clicquot. The excellent bubbly

# BIG NAME BUBBLES

made elsewhere in France does not have such high-profile brand names, although high-quality regional wines are well worth seeking out, such as Crémant d'Alsace, Crémant de Bourgogne from Burgundy, Blanquette de Limoux from Languedoc-Roussillon, sparkling Saumur and Vouvray from the Loire and Clairette de Die from near Grenoble.

Other Old World bubbly includes Cava from Spain, Sekt from Germany and Prosecco, Franciacorta and the deliciously sweet Asti from Italy. But the biggest revolution in sparkling wine has occurred in the New World, with wonderful Méthode Champenoise bubbly now being produced including Quartet and Mumm Cuvée Napa from California, Pelorus from New Zealand and the Australian-made Seaview and Taltarni. England's finest fizz is prize-winning Nyetimber. All worth a try!

From the huge photo-opportunity Nebuchadnezzars that require three or more people to lift them, to chic quarter-bottles drunk with a straw in trendy night-clubs, bubbly bottles are famous for their variety of sizes:

**Quarter-bottle** 20cl
**Half-bottle** 37.5cl
**Bottle** 75cl
**Magnum** 2 bottles
**Jeroboam** 4 bottles

**Rehoboam** 6 bottles
**Methuselah** 8 bottles
**Salmanazar** 12 bottles
**Balthazar** 16 bottles
**Nebuchadnezzar** 20 bottles

This short glossary might help make bubbly's terminology less confusing:

**Blanc de blancs** A white wine made solely from white grapes.

**Blanc de noirs** A white wine made solely from red grapes.

**Brut** Dry.

**Crémant** Wines that are only lightly sparkling.

**Demi-sec** Semi-sweet.

**Doux** Sweet.

**Extra brut** Very dry.

**Extra dry** Dry.

**Extra Sec** Dry.

**Mousse** The froth which fizzes in a glass of sparkling wine as it is poured.

**Mousseux** Sparkling.

**Non-Vintage (NV)** A blend of more than one vintage.

**Pétillant** Faintly sparkling.

**Sec** Medium-dry.

**Vintage** A wine of one particular year. Fine champagne vintages: 1985, 1988, 1990, 1995, 1996.

enjoy!

To impress the girls, Napoleon's officers would often slice off the tops of champagne bottles with their sabres, all very well early in the evening when their eye was true…

Notoriously, victorious Formula One drivers spray champagne into the crowds below, such exuberance both depressing the wine-maker and delighting the marketing men. With the pressure inside a bottle of bubbly being about 90lbs per square inch – roughly the same as the tyre pressure needed for a double-decker bus – it is little wonder that the cork pops out so easily, the longest flight of a cork being recorded at 177 feet 9 inches.

Unless you have just won a Grand Prix, the simplest way to open a bottle of bubbly is as follows:

1. Remove the foil and the wire from around the cork.

2. Hold the bottle at a slant, keeping the base in your strong hand and the cork in the other.

3. Twist the bottle slowly whilst holding the cork firmly (if you twist the cork, you risk it snapping).

4. Using the pressure inside the bottle to help you, ease the cork out gently. It should come out with a sigh rather than a bang, the noise of which would only draw attention to your enviable drinking habits and make your friends and neighbours jealous.

Bubbly is best served chilled, straight from a cool cellar or after just a couple of hours (rather than days) in the refrigerator. Alternatively, place the bottle inside an ice  bucket filled with a little ice and plenty of water. To pour, grasp the bottle by the base with your thumb inside the indentation. If it is your best bottle, ensure that the label points upwards so people can see what they are drinking, if it is your worst, make sure that it points downwards so they can't.

# JUST CHILL TO SERVE

Bubbly not only makes an ideal aperitif, it also goes well with caviar, rich pâtés, smoked salmon, gravadlax, oysters or lobster, whilst sweet bubbly is perfect with sweet soufflés, rich fruit cakes and strawberries and cream. It is also a crucial ingredient of some of the finest and most decadent cocktails, such as:

**Bellini**: ⅔ bubbly, ⅓ fresh peach juice.

**Black Velvet**: ½ bubbly, ½ draught Guinness.

**Buck's Fizz**: ⅔ bubbly, ⅓ fresh orange juice.

**Champagne Cocktail**: glass of champagne with the addition of a brandy-soaked sugar cube and a dash of Angostura bitters.

**Death in the afternoon**: ⅚ bubbly ⅙ pernod.

**Jojo**: ⅔ bubbly, ⅓ fresh strawberry juice.

**Kir Royale**: 1 glass of bubbly, crème de cassis to taste.

It is better to serve bubbly in 'tulips' or 'flutes' - elegant glasses which retain the wine's effervescence – as opposed to the shallow 'saucers' which allow the sparkle to dissipate too quickly. For the same reason it should be a criminal offence to use a 'swizzle-stick', an instrument designed to remove the fizz from champagne, thereby undoing the winemaker's painstaking efforts. If you want a still wine, buy a still wine, and leave the bubbles for us!

# ENJOY THE BUBBLES!

## PICTURE CREDITS

Key: **a**=above, **b**=below, **l**=left, **r**=right
1 photographer Peter Cassidy;
2 photographer Alan Williams;
3-13 photographer Peter Cassidy;
14 photographer Alan Williams;
17 photographer Peter Cassidy;
18 l Ruinart Champagne;
18 r & 19 Champagne Mumm;
21 al photographer Alan Williams;
21 b & r photographer Peter
Cassidy; 22-27 photographer
Peter Cassidy; 28-34 & 35 inset
photographer Alan Williams;
35 main photographer Peter
Cassidy; 36 photographer
Alan Williams; 37 & 38-39
photographer Peter Cassidy;
40 photographer Alan Williams;
43-64 photographer Peter Cassidy

The publisher and author would like to thank
all the businesses and home owners who
assisted us with the photography for this book.

PLACES TO BUY GLASSES AND OTHER BUBBLY
ACCESSORIES:

**The Conran Shop**
Michelin House, 81 Fulham Road, London SW3 6RD
t. 020 7589 7401
www.conranshop.co.uk

**Thomas Goode & Co.**
19 South Audley Street, London W1Y 6BN
t. 020 7499 2823
www.thomasgoode.co.uk

**Habitat**
196 Tottenham Court Road, London W1P 9LD
t. 0845 6010740 for branches
www.habitat.net

**Heal's**
196 Tottenham Court Road, London W1P 9LD
t. 020 7636 1666 for branches
www.heals.co.uk

**Purves & Purves**
80–81 & 83 Tottenham Court Road, London W1P 9HD
t. 020 7580 8223 for mail order
www.purves.co.uk

**Selfridges & Co.**
400 Oxford Street, London W1A 1AB
t. 020 7629 1234
www.selfridges.co.uk